a little

HANGOVER

CURES

Alex Benady

Appletree Press

First published in 1997 by
The Appletree Press Ltd,
The Old Potato Station,
14 Howard Street South,
Belfast BT7 1AP
Tel: +44 (0) 28 90 243074
Fax: +44 (0) 28 90 246756
E-mail: frontdesk@appletree.ie
Web Site: www.appletree.ie

Copyright © 1997 The Appletree Press Ltd.

A Little Book of Hangover Cures

A catalogue record for this book is
available from The British Library.

ISBN 0-86281-631-9

9 8 7 6 5 4 3 2 1

INTRODUCTION

No one knows for certain when alcohol was discovered - but it would be fair to assume that the hangover was discovered almost exactly ten hours later.

Imagine our noble ancestor's surprise. One minute he's strolling along as any good caveman does, swigging strangely fizzy water from a container that happened to hold some old fruit.

The next moment the world has become a rather droll and exciting place. Within an hour or two fellow cave inhabitants have become his dearest friends, and the mysteries of the universe are beginning to unfurl themselves. Later that night, happily chanting obscenities round the camp fire, he slips into a stupor and falls fast asleep.

Early next morning the fire has died and the cave is cold. Our caveman comes to, expecting last night's earthly paradise. But what's this?

He has been attacked. The bear who previously occupied the cave has returned and beaten him brutally around the head with a log. His eyes have been torn out and replaced with burning embers from the fire. And the contents of his bladder have been magically distributed all over his new fur coat.

3

As he tries to stand, our caveman notices in horror a sleeping figure lying next to him. In the cold light of day, the beautiful woman who seemed so sophisticated and alluring last night turns out to be a chimpanzee from the little group that hangs out over the next hill.

Poor *Homo sapiens*. For the sad fact is that, hideous though his current condition is, it's the best he is going to feel all day.

Actually, it's the best he's going to feel for the next two days because this caveman has, quite literally, The Mother Of All Hangovers. His skull is a little capsule of undiluted misery reverberating with drumming pains, pulsing pains, shooting pains and stabbing pains. His mouth is dry, caked with something unspeakable. In fact, he can't speak. His teeth feel as if they're made of suede. His tongue is swollen like a rotten salami and his breath tastes like a dog died in his throat two weeks ago.

Whenever he moves he thinks he's going to faint. When he turns his head, the world whirls by in a blur. His rebelliously squelchy stomach threatens to escape down his legs or rise up through his mouth.

His entire body shakes. His face and ears feel hot. His hands sweat while his torso feels clammy with cold.

Poor, poor *Homo sapiens*. He thought he'd discovered heaven. And in some ways he had. But at the same time he had also discovered hell. Could this have been man's first lesson in morality? Could it be that the fruit of the tree of wisdom was in fact a cider apple?

Alcohol certainly played an important religious role in early societies, where it was often used as a tool for philosophical enlightenment. And throughout history, man has been fascinated by the notion of dualism - the idea that everything contains its own opposite within. Day is followed by night, every high has its low, and yin has its yang just as surely as gin has its tonic.

In that sense this is an immoral tome. It is a blatant attempt to remove the pain from one of man's greatest pleasures. It is a blatant attempt to defy the fundamental laws of nature. It is a blatant attempt to cure the hangover.

CHAPTER ONE
A BRIEF HISTORY OF ALCOHOL

•••

Hundreds of thousands of years after the emergence of Homo sapiens were to slip by before man learnt to manufacture this magical liquid at will. But the moment he could, it seems he did - as much and as often as possible.

Some historians even believe that man ceased to be a wandering hunter-gatherer and became a settled farmer simply so that he could grow the grapes and grain that he needed to produce wine and beer. Whether this was the case or whether he was simply too hung over to walk, by 8000 BC inhabitants of the Middle East were worshipping the god of wild barley - the basic ingredient of beer. And within another thousand years, enthusiastic stone-age dipsomaniacs in the Caucasus were cultivating vines.

But the eternal shame of being the first named drunk in history falls to Noah, he of the ark and the flood. The book of Genesis tells us that after the flood:

"Noah began to be an husbandman, and he planted a vineyard..."

Fair enough, a bloke has to do something with his life. But by the next verse Noah had started consuming his own produce:

"… and he drank of the wine and was drunken..."

Worse still, he crashed out in a stupor, stark naked in his tent. It was left to his sons to shuffle backwards into the tent to cover him up, so they:

"...saw not their father's nakedness."

While the episode seems to have poisoned Noah's relationship with his sons, particularly with Ham, who discovered him in his compromised condition, it did his health no harm whatsoever. The Bible reports that Noah went on to live until he was 950 years old. Call me an infidel, but that seems unlikely even by Biblical standards. There must have been some kind of clerical error. Still, living to even 590 years as the result of drink sounds like a decent outcome.

If this is what people really believed at the time, it's hardly surprising that a slightly later writer, an anonymous Sumerian poet writing around 3000 BC, mused:

"I feel wonderful, drinking beer in a blissful mood, with joy in my heart and a happy liver."

Clearly the ancients still had much to learn both about poetry and the physical effects of alcohol. But beer in particular occupied a pivotal role in early civilisations - not only did it provide access to the spiritual world and a vital source of nourishment, it also lubricated the economy.

The Assyrians are said to have used beer, which they called kash, as a form of currency. To this day money is fondly known in drinking circles as beer tokens, and everywhere else as cash.

If anything, the ancient Egyptians were even more fond of a pint - economy and religion were inextricably linked and fuelled by what has lately been called 'the golden throat charmer'. Although to be strictly accurate Egyptian beer was almost certainly neither golden nor charming, but made from overcooked malt loaves to give it a dark brown colour, and mandrake - Shakespeare's insane root - to impart a bitter taste.

Wise old pharaoh Rameses realised that he who controls the beer controls the hearts and minds of the people. And so he established a state brewery - the first recorded example of any large-scale manufacturing enterprise undertaken by man - which enabled him to buy a round or two for his allies, most particularly the temple administrator, who received 10,000 hectolitres of free beer a year.

As the climate gradually grew warmer over the following millennia, grain gave way to vine around the Mediterranean - the focus of all the action at the time, at least on the European civilisation front.

The ancient Greeks in particular were well acquainted with the 'results of the rotten grape' - so much so, that, as we will see later, they became experts at developing strategies to deal with its consequences.

The Romans turned the Greek art of drinking into a religion - and not just for the men. The unique brand of spirituality of the maenads, female devotees of Bacchus, the god of pleasure, took the form of mammoth drinking frenzies which invariably culminated in a sexual free-for-all. And as it was also the Romans who pioneered the use of lead as an additive to sweeten their wine - a habit which persisted until it was banned last century - it is likely that these drunken exhibitionists suffered from particularly heavy hangovers.

Now the Romans may have loved their wine, but like many who followed them, they were revolted by British beer. The emperor Julian was so moved by his first taste of what was presumably a warm, flat, yeasty concoction, that he wrote a little ditty about it. He called it *On Wine Made from Barley*.

> "Who made you and from what?
> By the true Bacchus I know you not
> He smells of nectar, But you smell of goat."

But even 'Eau de Goat' has its uses, and the Romans soon pressed it into service as a tonic and vitamin supplement to combat outbreaks of tuberculosis among the legionaries.

If the maenads had taken the trouble, they would have also found that it was an excellent cure for thrush.

And so British beer continued on its merry way, impervious to the insults of the invader.

During the Dark Ages, brewing was primarily a domestic process carried out by women. When a new brew was ready they would place a leaf-covered pole in the window to advertise the fact. This was the genesis of the English pub, and explains why pub signs are still hung from poles, and why so many feature the word 'bush' in their name.

With the advent of Christianity, beer making became a guy thing and a religious thing once more. The monasteries had enormous brewing operations. At the time of the Domesday Book, the brothers of St Paul's Cathedral in London produced an average of two hundred gallons of ale a day. Having said that, the brothers saw eight pints a day as the basic requirement for human life - so by the standards of the time perhaps it wasn't such a big deal.

For the next thousand years or so, Europeans sank quantities of alcohol which in this namby-pamby age would immediately mark them out as having a serious problem. But did they let it interfere with their work? Not for a moment. Even the early growth of the British Empire can be attributed to drink.

Until 1740, British sailors were allowed half a pint of neat rum per day. Which explains two things: why they discovered so many new lands as they lurched drunkenly round the globe - (they were constantly lost), and the extreme aggression which allowed them to take over when they got there.

Things weren't much better on the continent. Philip the Handsome of Spain was a noted drunkard and, like many other monarchs and popes, drank himself to death. Nothing particularly amusing or clever about that. Unusually, though, his wife Joanna joined him in bed for a last snifter as he lay dying, and never quite sobered up sufficiently to get out again. In fact she sprawled there for the next three years, attempting to run the country in between drinking toasts to her dead husband, whose putrefying corpse she insisted should remain by her side. One can only admire such loyalty. But legend has it that when Phil's sticky remains were finally removed, his loving and by now totally insane queen didn't even notice.

"There is no cure for a hangover save death."

Robert Benchley

In the ninth century an anonymous Arab developed the first still (the apparatus used for carrying out distillation) or *kuhl*, which in time gave alcohol its name. Paradoxically, the rise of Islam represented the first major reverse for alcohol and its dark shadow, the hangover, as the outlawing of drink gradually turned great swathes of the middle and near East into hangover-free zones.

The only other comparably alcohol-free area on earth was pre-Columbian North America. Here, for reasons not entirely clear, but possibly related to the inhabitants' preference for hallucinogens and narcotics, whole generations failed to discover fermentation. Although the Papago of the south west developed a cactus wine and the Tarahumara of New Mexico are said to have brewed a decent drop of corn beer, the rest of the continent remained as dry as James Bond's martini.

The New World continued its ambivalent relationship with drink right into the twentieth century. Nowhere was this more evident than during the Prohibition, that bizarre and self-defeating outbreak of misplaced civic morality, which, far from reducing the amount of drinking and attendant immorality, had exactly the opposite effect. People found all sorts of ingenious ways around the ban. One distiller, RA Dickel of Kentucky, simply had its proprietary bourbon redesignated as a medicine and made available on prescription, while some drinkers slaked their thirst aboard boats that cruised just outside territorial waters. Illegal drinking clubs blossomed like flowers after a desert rain.

After ten years of Prohibition, the consumption of alcohol soared; organised crime became wealthy beyond its wildest dreams, and breaking the law had become commonplace. And what's more, the hangover (the word had only entered the language thirty years earlier), had now become a status symbol and an amusing mark of world-weary sophistication.

CHAPTER TWO
THE BODY OF EVIDENCE

●●●

You may well be reading this book in a spirit of scientific enquiry. Perhaps you seek to broaden your horizons in areas where you have no first-hand experience, or maybe you want to gain insight into the plight of those less fortunate than yourself.

Far more likely, however, is that you are a habitual drunkard in the grip of a violent and very painful hangover and you are desperately seeking respite. But before you can have salvation, you must understand the nature of your damnation.

A hangover is an invisible enemy. It has penetrated your body's defences and is insidiously wreaking havoc on a whole range of key systems at once - making it hard, but not impossible, to remedy.

The major problem is one of toxic attack, as your body has only limited ability to process poisons. When you drink, enzymes in your liver break down the alcohol first into acetaldehyde, a hideous toxin far worse than alcohol, and then into a comparatively benign substance called acetate. The process is aided by a friendly chemical known as nicotinic acid derivative (NAD), which helps the metabolising of both the alcohol and the acetaldehyde.

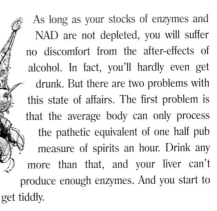

As long as your stocks of enzymes and NAD are not depleted, you will suffer no discomfort from the after-effects of alcohol. In fact, you'll hardly even get drunk. But there are two problems with this state of affairs. The first problem is that the average body can only process the pathetic equivalent of one half pub measure of spirits an hour. Drink any more than that, and your liver can't produce enough enzymes. And you start to get tiddly.

The second problem is that most drinks are not pure alcohol. They have all sorts of additives, colourings and flavourings to make them more interesting. It's these little extras that do all the serious damage. Known as congeners, they can include substances which if taken neat would kill you stone dead. Diluted in alcohol they will merely make you wish you were dead.

But all is not lost - several defensive strategies are at hand. For starters, you could try to limit your intake of alcohol to the level that the body can metabolise. This approach has only limited appeal as it involves drinking much less, more slowly. Another, easier tactic is to inhibit the absorption of alcohol in the first place by lining the stomach walls with fat and oil before you start drinking.

You could also choose drinks with fewer congeners. Broadly speaking, the purer, or lighter colour, the bevvy, the fewer congeners it contains, which explains why bourbon, brandy and port are the worst offenders while vodka and white wine are comparatively innocent.

But suppose for a moment you have been rash enough to allow a glass or two of red wine or sherry - both bristling with congeners - on board. What are your options?

You could try a chemical defence in the form of chelators - chemical grabbers which attach themselves to the congeners and take them away. Charcoal, cabbage and vitamin C are all well known chelators:

> "Last evening you were drinking deep,
> So now your head aches. Go to sleep.
> Take some boiled cabbage when you wake
> And there's an end to your head ache."

Athenaeus - Banquet of the Learned

Boosting your ability to metabolise the toxins is another defence: fructose (found in honey, for example) and oxygen are said to be useful tools for this. And one good way to get oxygen into your blood is exercise.

This provides the physiological basis for the good shag school of hangover cures:

"Upon wakening if your wife or other partner is beside you, and (of course) is willing, perform the sexual act as vigorously as you can. The exercise will do you good, and - on the assumption that you enjoy sex - you will feel toned up emotionally."

Kingsley Amis

So now you think the battle is won - but there's another problem. Alcohol is a depressant. The brain responds by altering its cell walls to cope with the onslaught. But the brain adapts more slowly than the alcohol recedes. So next morning your poor brain is still trying to deal with large amounts of poison that aren't there. And the outcome? An extreme sensitivity to noise, light and movement that characterises the early stages of a hangover:

"Can't anyone do something about that racket?"

Bibulous superhero **WC Fields**, on hearing the fizzing of Alka Seltzer in a glass after a particularly heavy night.

Your brain is screaming to be let down gently. It needs to be eased, teased and coaxed lovingly back into sobriety, not pushed callously into the deep end. This is the physiological basis for the hair of the dog, dismissed by many as a myth. In fact, a small nip from the animal that bit you will allow your brain to edge its way gingerly back to normality.

"I was left in no doubt as to the severity of the hangover when a cat stamped into the room."

PG Wodehouse

Apart from having sunk fifteen pints, the reason why you need to urinate so much when you have been drinking is that alcohol is a powerful diuretic - the body has no choice in the matter, it must pass water.

And as well as dehydrating you, alcohol also destroys a whole range of vital salts, vitamins and trace elements - your stocks of calcium, potassium, magnesium, vitamin C, B1 and B6 all take a severe pasting after a few drinks. This, plus the effects of two packs of high tar cigarettes and a bucketful of finest vindaloo curry, explains why your mouth often tastes like a compost heap the next morning.

Alcohol also causes your insulin production to go into overdrive, reducing blood sugar levels and adding to feelings of faintness, fatigue and hunger.

Fortunately, the remedy for dehydration, vitamin loss and chemical imbalance is simple - make sure you replace liquids and other substances, preferably before a session, and certainly early the next day:

"While beer brings gladness, don't forget that water only makes you wet."

Harry Leon Wilson

There's just one last problem - an outbreak of extreme torpor and lassitude. That pernicious poison interferes with what is known as REM, or rapid eye movement, the part of sleep in which you dream. REM occurs four or five times a night. Without it you become at first irritable, and after a few days a fully functioning freely-hallucinating psychotic.

Your system copes with lack of REM by producing dreams of its own, during the day if necessary. It doesn't care if at the time you happen to be driving, talking to your boss or hearing a confession.

"Why has the good old custom of coming together to get drunk gone out? Think of the delight of drinking in pleasant company and then lying down to a deep long sleep."

Nathaniel Hawthorne

Even those readers who are not rocket scientists will recognise the implications of this. After drinking (preferably in company), try to get to bed early (preferably alone), and stay there for as long as possible.

Of course, all this merely describes the forces at work within your body. The precise outcome in terms of pain experienced for a given amount of alcohol drunk varies from individual to individual, according to his or her physical and emotional make-up.

A key factor is how experienced a drinker you are. Obviously, if you've been putting away two bottles of cheap red every night - for the last five years, a few cups of sangria aren't going to sort you out in quite the same way that they might finish off a complete novice.

A great deal also depends on how large you are. The relationship between alcohol capacity and size is fairly direct. So, other things being equal, a sixteen- stone man will have precisely the same amount of blood stream alcohol after four pints as will an eight-stone woman after two.

That's pretty much all you need to know about what constitutes a hangover and what symptoms any remedy must address. Armed with this knowledge, you'll be able to discern a faint glimmer of scientific rationale for many of the outlandish fetishes and rituals that follow.

• HANGOVER RATING OF DIFFERENT DRINKS •

BOURBON 10/10	You're better off dead. In fact, you may already be dead.
PORT 9/10	Perhaps intensive care isn't such a bad place after all.
SHERRY 8/10	Anyway, it's cool to have your stomach pumped.
RED WINE 8/10	Stomach pumps prove very popular.
PURE MALT 7/10	Book your season ticket for desolation row.
CHAMPAGNE 7/10	Desolation row next stop.
BRANDY 6/10	Nothing that three hundred aspirin and two days off work won't sort out.
RUM 6/10	Visit the chemist & continue your 'sick leave'.
SCOTCH 5/10	This would put most people off drink for life, but not you.
WHITE WINE 4/10	Perhaps you wouldn't feel so crap now if you'd bothered to eat something.
BEER 3/10	You may be able to live with the hangover, but will you be able to live with the gut that comes from drinking beer in these quantities?
GIN 2/10	Let this be a warning.
VODKA 1/10	You think you're so clever. You may have escaped a hangover but cyrrhosis doesn't show up until it's too late.

CHAPTER THREE

ANTI-HANGOVER STRATEGIES &
A CAUTIONARY TALE

• • •

Think of the smattering of physiological knowledge you've just acquired as building blocks from which you'll construct the edifice which is your anti-hangover strategy.

Logic dictates that there are five basic ways to deal with a hangover:

1. AVOID IT
You don't have to drink. There's always the sober option. Just say no. This route has the advantage of being the only sure-fire way known to man to escape hangovers. But even an intellectual pygmy like Dean Martin could spot the major flaw in this approach:

"I feel sorry for people who don't drink. When they wake up in the morning that's as good as they are going to feel all day long."

2. PREVENT IT
Prevention is a jolly sensible approach. Unfortunately, prevention also involves active stewardship of one's body during a drinking session, through measures such as ingesting water and vitamins. If you're capable of such interventions it probably means you are not properly drunk and wouldn't have had much of a hangover anyway.

3. ENDURE IT

This is the approach favoured by sadists and high-handed moralists. It contains the loathsome implication that your actions are your responsibility and that you should bear the consequences. But perhaps there's a tiny bit of puritan in all of us - and maybe it does us good to do penance for having a good time by punishing our souls, heads, stomachs and so forth every now and then.

"The only way to get rid of temptation is to yield to it."

Oscar Wilde

4. ANAESTHETISE IT

You can always numb your pain with a medicine cabinet full of aspirin, paracetamol, Quaaludes and silver polish. While this is by far the most popular approach, its major disadvantage is that it doesn't actually address any of your real symptoms. It also leaves your body as trashed as it was before the cure, if not more so.

5. DEAL WITH IT

If you're the sort of person whose financial planning consists of £10 on a dead cert in the 3pm at Newbury, or if you believe that the lottery is going to solve all your problems - if, in other words, you are a typical drinker, then this the course of action for you. It is otherwise known as having your cake and eating it.

Just take full responsibility for your drinking and your hangover and hope that among all the cures that follow there is one that will magically relieve all your symptoms and effortlessly restore you to perfect good health.

But a word of warning before we proceed: So far this book has reflected the widely held belief that a hangover is a mild inconvenience - a price worth paying for the occasional night of merriment. To get a different and perhaps a more accurate perspective on the hangover, forget for a moment that booze was the culprit and try and imagine your reaction to someone who had taken too much of another dangerous drug last night, such as heroin.

YOU: God, you look awful. You must have really tied one on last night.

FRIEND (clutching head in self-pitying manner): Several, actually. And I used your best tie as a tourniquet. Sorry about the blood stains. Yeah, we got half a gram of Chinese rocks and shot it all up in an hour. Trouble was it was cut with potassium permanganate and we had to share a syringe between three of us. Boy, did we OD.

Do you: a) Laugh in conspiratorial but sympathetic fashion and start preparing your buddy a clean syringe full of your own pure 'gear'? or b) Immediately call the police, an ambulance and a psychiatrist, in that order? Anyway, enough moralising. Let's party.

Chapter Four
Around the World in a Daze

●●●

Pay a visit to any fashionable restaurant almost anywhere in the world and you'll find that this season the *beau monde* and *jeunesse dorée* are no longer getting legless at lunchtime. Contemporary health concerns mean that extreme drunkenness, especially in the afternoon, is just a little unhip and politically incorrect.

There's a certain irony in this because in many ways the hangover is the very model of an equal opportunities institution. It doesn't give a damn about sex, creed, colour or political conviction – we are all blades of grass to be felled without distinction by its mighty scythe.

Unless of course you happen to be Japanese, in which case it is said that the balance of enzymes in your system means that you are far more susceptible to the ravages of alcohol than the rest of us. The national sensitivity to alcohol is perfectly reflected in the Japanese expression for a hangover, *futska yoi*, literally, two days drunk.

Nearly every language has its own colourful phrases for this universal trauma. Cat and wood themes are especially popular. So the Germans experience a *katzenjammer* or 'a wailing of cats', the Dutch are subject to *kater* or 'noisy cats', while the Poles merely have to cope with *kociokwik*, the 'moaning of kittens'.

The French are afflicted by a *gueule de bois*, 'a wooden palate'. In Denmark you might be attacked by *tommermaend*, or 'carpenters', and in Norway you will be hit by *jeg har tommermen*, 'carpenters in the head'. The oh so literal Swedes settle for *Hont i haret*, a 'pain in the root of the hair'.

The Latins, feeling less guilty about their pleasures, tend to more direct expressions of their discomfort. The Italians favour *malessere dopo una sbornia*, 'sickness after a piss-up', and the Spanish and Portuguese content themselves with the simple but apt word *resaca*, or 'surge'.

The cures themselves are a mixture of science, common sense, wishful thinking, superstition and total cobblers.

THE AUSSIE BELLY BUSTER

As the heaviest beer drinkers in the world, Australians know a thing or two about hangovers. An Australian doctor describes the perfect prophylactic (preventative) meal as a bowl of milk and cornflakes (packed with vitamin B) and a whole orange (for vitamin C), followed by a plate of well-salted potatoes mashed with butter and a glass of full-cream milk (to line the stomach).

The Hot to Trot (Netherlands)

Take a liver (a cow's, not your own), sheep's trotters and oatmeal. Boil them up for six hours and strain. This, er, delicious sounding soup is another comfort food high in proteins and carbohydrates. Just the job if you're a seventeenth-century peasant who wants to stay that way.

Irish Breakfast

Half a dozen oysters and a pint of Guinness are recommended as a little tonic in Ireland. Guinness is loaded with all sorts of minerals and foodie things to restore your body's natural balance as well as alcohol to ease your brain and dissolve your pain. The oysters are said to contain zinc.

The Sauna (Finland)

The heat will get your circulation going and help you to sweat some of the toxins out of your system. The optional roll in the snow will give your body a good metaphorical slapping which should help shake off any residual fatigue. However, beware if you are very dehydrated - few recorded cases of extreme heat have helped this condition. And don't be tempted to smash a bottle of vodka in the sauna - you should have done that the night before

The Voodoo Cure (Haiti)

Not a promising cure, this. Stick thirteen black-headed pins into the bottle from which you've been drinking. If you've more than one bottle, at least the concentration required to manipulate twenty-six, thirty-nine, fifty-two or more pins will take your mind off your suffering for a while.

THE PUERTO RICAN FAITH CURE

This cure is only one step removed from the ascorbic acid suppository. Slice a ripe lemon in half and rub firmly into your armpits. American raconteur and writer Waverley Root noted this (supposed) cure in an article in the New York Times nearly twenty years ago. Was he serious? Does it work? Comments to W Root, c/o New York Times, New York.

THE PRAIRIE OYSTER (US)

Wranglers and cow hands like nothing more than a plate of fried bull's testicles after a hard day's castratin'. For obvious reasons they call them prairie oysters. This recipe, you'll be relieved to hear, calls for no bull whatsoever.

Ingredients:

1 egg yolk, 1 tablespoonful of Worcestershire sauce
1/2 oz port, celery salt, freshly ground pepper

Pour all the ingredients into a wine glass. Try not to break the yolk. Down in one.

THE POST HOCK (GERMANY)

In Germany they like to do things scientifically. None of your superstitious eating-lizard's-gizzards-on-the-fifth-Tuesday-of-a-leap-year nonsense for them. They want a remedy that is reliable, proven and which will run on time. In terms of addressing your physiological symptoms this cure is one of the best there is - even if it is rather lacking that vital ingredient, compassion.

Seek out a co-operative chemist and ask him for a glass containing gentle pain relief, vitamin B complex, and loads of vitamin C, all in an alkaline mix. It will ease pain, rehydrate, replace lost vits and mins and settle your stomach.

THE HERRING AID (GERMANY)

Before they had science in Germany, they had fish. The herring is attributed with almost mythical anti-hangover properties by its supporters.

CABBAGE SOUP (RUSSIA)

To many it seems as if the entire Soviet nation gets as drunk as a skunk on a regular basis. But as people drink mostly vodka, which is very low in impurities, Russians generally don't get the hangovers you may feel they richly deserve. However, if they do down the odd gallon of plum brandy or radioactive slurry by mistake, the cleansing effect of the chelators in the cabbage makes this soup an excellent cure.

Ingredients:

1 lb lean beef and a marrow bone
1 clove garlic, 1 carrot, celery, bay leaf, pepper
half a cabbage, fresh dill, sour cream, salt.

Boil it all then drink it all.

THE MONT BLANC (SWITZERLAND)

Otherwise known as the snowball from hell. This doesn't really come from Switzerland, just that the egg white and ice make it look a bit alpine. It is a hair of the dog cure par excellence which settles the stomach and restores sugar levels.

Ingredients:
1 measure vermouth
2 measures absinthe
half a teaspoon of syrup
1 whisked egg white
Add ice and shake well. Top up with soda water.

THE RED DEVIL (UK)

If there's one thing they love in Manchester more than their ale, it's their football. If you're a Mancunian this cure has the great advantage of being able to dress your favourite tipple in Man United colours.

To a pint glass add one half pint of bitter (Boddington's for that authentic taste), and one half pint of tomato juice. Wave around stylishly in front of mouth and then spill dramatically all over left shoulder in a bold attempt to mimic the playing style of your footballing heroes.

JAMAICA SURPRISE

This is just about as sensuous and cosseting a posset you'll ever find. Treat your poor defiled body to this smooth rich elixir and know the meaning of the word recovery. The surprise sometimes comes fifteen minutes later when your belly decides it was too much of a good thing and rejects it.

Ingredients:
1 measure single rum
1 teaspoon honey
1 teaspoon double cream
Mix everything and shake with lots of ice.

THE EYEBALL TO EYEBALL (OUTER MONGOLIA)

One of the problems in researching a book like this is that your sources may not always stand up to the most rigorous scrutiny. I don't know anyone who could verify this cure, but what the hell, it sounds interesting.

Should you ever find yourself suffering from a surfeit of fermented yak's milk, take a pickled sheep's eye from the jar which you keep in your yurt specially for this purpose, pop it in a glass and fill with tomato juice. Stare manfully into the glass until one of you blinks, then down the horrid beverage in one. This cure is so revolting that your hangover will soon seem trivial by comparison.

THE WHALE BONE POSSET (MOROCCO)

I discovered this traditional cure in the Djemaa el Fna, the grand square of Marrakesh. It was told to me in person by a proud Berber warrior and medicine man, his leathery face as lined and cracked as the ageless rocks of the desert, his bloodshot eyes glinting like rubies in the smoky night air.

Take bone of whale, which after some years becomes spongy and easily powdered, and burn it in a small crucible. The resulting smoke will vanquish the demons and restore you to a state of grace.

I was subsequently advised that many of the so-called Berber shamen in the square are in fact engineering students from the University of Casablanca earning extra holiday money. But I don't feel that this compromises the integrity of the cure by one jot.

THE GREAT BRITISH FRY UP

Foreigners are usually appalled by what passes muster as food in Britain. In fact they often pass laws against it. But even in the desolate wastes of British cuisine, the Great British Fry Up stands out like a beacon in the night when it comes to the sheer poor quality of ingredients used and the artless, witless way in which they are cooked and combined.

But for reasons unknown this symphony of cholesterol, this rhapsody in lard exercises an uncanny power over Britons, all of whom, from the very highest in the land to the very lowest, swear by its amazing curative powers.

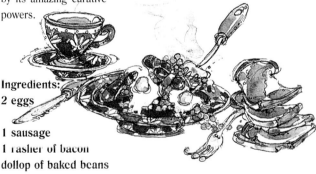

Ingredients:
2 eggs

1 sausage
1 rasher of bacon
dollop of baked beans
black pudding, fried tomatoes and mushrooms to taste
white toast
1 nice cup of splosh

Fry everything (except for the tea).

CHAPTER FIVE
THE LESSONS OF HISTORY

● ● ●

What is it about hangover cures that have inspired man to commit them to paper, clay, stone, leather and anything else he could mark?

Was it the feeling that like the secret of eternal life, a good hangover cure allows you to defy the laws of nature? Or was it simply that mankind has an eye for a bargain and the possibility of getting drunk without paying the penalty seems too good not to shout about?

Whatever the reason, history provides us with an almost endless fount of wisdom on the subject of hangover cures. And not all of it is complete nonsense.

THE ASSYRIAN BEAK DUST CURE

Apart from inventing the electrical battery and the word 'cash', the Assyrians made one other significant gift to posterity - they were the first to set down a hangover cure in writing. According to clay tablets discovered last century in the city of Nineveh, they recommended crushed swallows' beaks mixed with myrrh as the cure for overindulgence.

This may sound like primitive nonsense to modern ears. But as swallows' beaks are made of calcium, which the body needs to replace after a protracted drinking session, you could argue that the Assyrian cure does contain at least a grain of sense.

Which is more than can be said for early Greek remedies. They were the first to employ scientific methods in search of an effective hangover cure, but initial attempts were little more than stabs in the dark. Routine hangover prevention measures for the serious ancient Greek drinker included wearing purple and drinking out of amethyst-encrusted goblets.

But as great empiricists, the Greeks didn't hang around. The moment these methods proved to be useless - within a couple of hundred years at most - they'd moved on to more sophisticated approaches.

THE HAIR OF THE GREEK DOG

This has the triple distinction of being the second oldest recorded hangover cure, of having stood the test of time, and of being written in verse. What's more it makes a lot more sense than the colour purple:

"Take the hair, it is well written
Of the dog by which you're bitten
Work off one wine by his brother
One labour by another."

Antiphanes, 479 BC

THE HEIR OF THE HAIR OF THE DOG

Many would later try to claim Antiphanes's cure as their own, including a sixteenth-century Englishman called John Heywood who wrote:

> "I pray thee let me and my fellow have
> A haire of the dog that bit us last night."

Various writers have subsequently suggested that the word 'hair' be replaced by 'hairs', or even 'tuft'. Some have taken this piece of folk wisdom as an excuse to experiment with the entire 'pelt' of the dog. However, they should be warned that there is a difference between curing a hangover and getting paralytic again. If you find the distinction too fine to make, you probably need medical help.

THE GREEK SEA SICKNESS CURE

The Greeks also stumbled upon a cure even more effective than the hair of the dog. It was called being sick. The later Greeks would prevent hangovers by the brilliantly simple expedient of adding sea water to their wine, which would make them vomit, stopping them from getting drunk in the first place.

PLINY'S SHEET STAINER

A noted Roman, Pliny the Elder, was the first man to make a systematic study of hangover cures. Initially he recommended wearing a garland of parsley to bed after a heavy session to ward off any ill effects. Sadly, this merely resulted in green stains being added to the technicolour spectrum of all the other stains on the sheets of those who tried it. In later life he abandoned this remedy in favour of the thoroughly modern and sensible practice of swallowing raw eggs and drinking olive oil and garlic.

THE ROMAN CANDLE CURE

So called because it was a Roman favourite and used sheep's lights, or lungs as we now know them. Lately it has become better known as The Silence of the Lamb's Cure. It can be prepared in many ways, but the simplest is to make what can only be described as sheep's lung sausages.

These days it is often simpler to buy lungs at the butcher or supermarket rather than bothering with all the mess of brutally slaughtering your fluffy pet lamb.

But if you prefer the traditional method, take your sheep and stab it in the throat with a sharp metal implement. Wait until it's quite dead. Skin it. Then rip out its lungs and some of the large intestine and stuff the former into the latter. Grill or barbecue to taste.

THE EGYPTO-ROMAN CABBAGE CURE

The Egyptians used to eat large amounts of cabbage hors d'oeuvres at their feasts, while the Romans used it as a post-binge restorative. Science confirms the efficacy of the humble cabbage as a hangover cure. So full marks to the Germans who like to eat sauerkraut while drinking.

GENGHIS KHAN'S CURE

This doesn't have anything to do with the great warrior king, but it does include cream of tartar, allowing a weak and inaccurate pun to be made in the name.

Ingredients:
1 teaspoon Epsom salts
1 teaspoon cream of tartar
1 teaspoon ground ginger

Mix ingredients and dissolve in water. This is a sensible refreshing tonic that will calm the stomach and replace lost minerals. It will dent a middleweight hangover but will not cut the mustard when it comes to serious alcoholic poisoning.

THE MERRYE OLDE ENGLANDE CURE

In days of old when knights were bold and aspirin wasn't invented, they chopped almonds and eel into their breakfast grog and spent the day well contented.

BOYLE'S HEID-AKE CURE

Robert Boyle was a seventeenth-century scientist famous for Boyle's Law, which states that at a given temperature, pressure in a gas varies inversely with volume.

Contrast that precise insight with his *'After Drinking Cure for the Heid-ake'*:

"Take green hemlock that is tender, and put them in your socks, so that it may lie thinly between them and the soles of your feet: shift the herbs once a day."

RABBIT DROPPINGS TEA

This is a cure from the days of the Wild West when men were men and they often owned land for as far as they could see. Which would be just about to the end of their toes, because whiskey in those days often wasn't so much whiskey as paint stripper, creosote, weak coffee or anything else brown, wet, and toxic.

But if you did get blind drunk and had the foresight to take precautions, you would have gathered plenty of jackrabbit droppings and dried them. On waking from your stupor you would mix them into a tea and drink a cup every half hour.

THE BLACK AND WHITE CURE

Victorian chimney sweeps in London really did use this cure. What's more, lawks alive and god bless yer sir, it really worked.

Ingredients:
1 cup of warm milk
1 level teaspoon of soot

Mix everything and drink slowly. The warm milk will rehydrate you, restore some of the lost minerals, and ease the stomach. The soot or charcoal is a chelator and will help your body dispose of all the poisons left over from last night.

BAUME DE FLORIANI

Baume de Floriani was a blend of white wine, turpentine and spices which became a hugely popular hangover cure in Italy last century. It's hard to imagine why. Under no circumstances try to make this at home.

CHAPTER SIX
CURES OF THE FAMOUS

●●●

For some reason the famous people who have donated their hangover cures to posterity tend to be the creative sort - writers, actors and media types. Why have so few engineers, clerks, rat catchers, accountants, lawyers and metal lathe turners contributed to the literature? It certainly isn't because they don't get hangovers.

HEMINGWAY'S BLOODY MARY
Strictly speaking, this is just a cocktail. But the nourishment of the tomato juice combined with the hair of the dog drop of vodka make it an excellent restorative for the more advanced drinker.

Ingredients:
1 part vodka
7 parts tomato juice
drop of Tabasco
2 drops of Worcestershire sauce
lemon juice
salt and pepper to taste.

The drink is said to have been named after Queen Mary Tudor. But as sixteenth century England was not exactly awash with vodka, or Tabasco for that matter, it must have been a long time after.

A much better story is that Ernest Hemingway, who used to drink at Harry's Bar in New York, once used tomato juice to conceal from his wife Mary the fact that he was drinking vodka. It worked a treat, and next day the distinguished writer confided in the barman: 'We've caught her out, that bloody Mary.'

PEPYS'S CURE

The eighteenth century London diarist Samuel Pepys was a noted dipso, constantly battling with the bottle. As one of the most opinionated men in the history of the universe it would be astonishing if he had nothing to say on the subject of hangovers and cures. Needless to say, Samuel failed to astonish on this count.

His suggestions include drinking whey, horseradish, ale and turpentine. When sober, he once recommended this eminently sensible remedy:

Pour ample sugar into a quart of orange juice.

It has loads of vitamin C, loads of energy, and a sufficient volume of liquid to rehydrate you.

WALTER MATTHAU

Ice Cream. This is a sensible and soothing remedy recommended by a man who looks like he was born with a hangover. 'I was drunk once', he confessed. 'It was 1943 in Kearney, Nebraska. I tried ice cream to get over the hangover, but that didn't work so I just suffered until the ice cream would stay down.'

F SCOTT FITZGERALD

According to a biography of this Olympic-standard tippler, Fitzgerald wrote this cure for a friend who had requested that he write something special for her:

'I have never scene Skot Fisgurel sober but he is a grate freind of mine. He has offen toled me about his methods. He begins in the mawning with 3 (three) strong whiskies and from then on for years and years he seldom stops.'

WC FIELDS

The F Scott Fitzgerald approach sounds remarkably similar to that adopted by his thespian contemporary, WC Fields. But whereas Fitzgerald at least pretended to be slightly ashamed of his 'problem', Fields was constantly on the attack and remained unapologetic about his immoderate consumption, right to the bottom of his glass. When asked if he wanted a glass of water he once replied: 'Watah, fish f*** in watah!' Which I think we can interpret as a 'no'.

Instead he preferred a martini made of one part vermouth to four parts gin - taken around the clock.

THE EVELYN WAUGH CAUGH

The English writer Evelyn Waugh (pronounced War), best known as author of *Brideshead Revisited*, was a fearful snob and a chest beating class warrior.

Drink played an important part in the lives of the indolent aristocracy with whom he aspired to rub shoulders and so it is inconceivable that he should choose anything other than champagne as the main ingredient of his cure.

Ingredients: 1 glass champagne,1 cube sugar Angostura bitters, red pepper.

Dunk a sugar cube in Angostura bitters and dust with red pepper. Drop it into the champagne and drink after a few moments' contemplation. Waugh described it as painfully delicious. I would describe it as just painful.

KEITH FLOYD'S WINE POSSET

Globetrotting English oenophile and TV chef Keith Floyd makes no secret of his fondness for a glass or five. In fact, he has made a career out of it. There can be few men alive with his experience of drinks from all over the world and the opportunity to experiment with corrective measures. If a university were ever to establish a chair of Applied Hangoverology, Mr Floyd would be the man to sit in it.

He describes this as a treatment for a slight head after too much wine…which not only works wonders, but is also extremely delicious. Interestingly, he gives quantities for two people. As you are probably not a TV personality and therefore unlikely to be entertaining overnight, adjust measures accordingly.

Ingredients: 1 tumbler milk,1 tumbler dry white wine, 1 dessertspoonful runny honey, 1 teaspoonful of finely grated lemon zest, pinch each of ground ginger, cloves, cinnamon and freshly grated nutmeg.

Heat the milk and wine together until the milk has curdled, sprinkle with spices, strain into two glasses and drink while warm.

KEITH RICHARDS

This is the man who can truly be said to have launched a thousand serious drink problems. In his heyday, the Rolling Stones guitarist was renowned as the most elegantly wasted man on earth. Many tried to copy his dishevelled hedonism, forgetting that they had neither his astonishingly robust constitution nor his astonishingly robust bank balance.

Keith, who for twenty years was rarely photographed without a bottle of Jack Daniels in hand, had remarkably simple ways of coping with the fallout from a major league bender. Sometimes he would just have his blood changed. More often he would retire to his bed for one, two or even three days until the problem had passed.

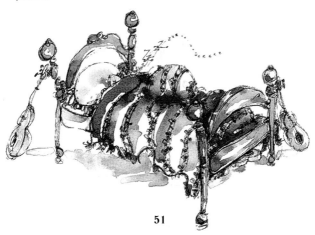

CHAPTER SEVEN
NEW AGE AND PROPRIETARY CURES

• • •

Most people may not believe in witchcraft any more, but they have replaced it in their explanation of the universe with an astonishing array of nostrums, postulations, credos and flights of fancy. Which means that today, despite our scientific sophistication, there is probably a wider range of hangover cures than ever before. Some represent the extreme limits of wishful thinking. Others just represent the extreme limits of commercial opportunism.

REFLEXOLOGY
Based on the belief that the body is mirrored in the foot. Tightly squeeze your big toe just under the first knuckle with your thumb and forefinger for two minutes, and *voilà* - no headache, they say.

NUX VOMICA
This is an old homeopathic cure which combats the poisons in your system with just a hint of strychnine. Clears the head and stomach. Don't under any circumstances be tempted to save money by making your own.

MEADOWSWEET
A common herb containing a natural form of salicylate, the active ingredient in aspirin. Just find a field of the stuff and graze till you feel better.

English readers may prefer to chew their cricket bats on the grounds that they are made of willow which contains even more salicylate.

AROMATHERAPY

Evening primrose oil when massaged into the skin is said to have remarkable rejuvenative effects, while peppermint stimulates the system and eucalyptus clears the head. This cure is at its most potent if you employ a young masseur of the opposite sex and merge it seamlessly with the Kingsley Amis remedy (see Chapter 2).

BRAIN MACHINES

The product of the marriage between leading edge technology and belief in fairies, these headset-like devices work by producing visual and aural stimuli that are designed to copy the pattern of your brain activity. Half an hour in one of them made a discernible difference to one of the worst hangovers I have ever had. Highly recommended.

JAPANESE CORAL SAND

When used as a teabag style infusion, it is said to take the acidity out of liquids. However, dumping half the continental shelf of Japan into your pint also takes the fun out of drinking. This is one for the very gullible only.

ALKA-SELTZER

The best known proprietary cure of all. Containing aspirin, citric acid and sodium bicarbonate, it will deal with your headache and help your stomach.

This is a reliable if uninspired cure that should help with all but the very worst post-alcohol traumas.

MORNING AFTER

Made by Country House Products of Great Britain, it is described as 'the first natural hangover comforter'. Notice that they don't call it a cure, so full marks for honesty. It comes in teabag form and contains extracts of just about every plant that ever grew. Drink a pint of this genteel, restorative brew before retiring. Personally, I'd rather bite the heads off little baby bunny rabbits and drink their blood.

FERNET BRANCA AND UNDERBERG

I bracket these two peculiar little tonics together, even though one is a bitter liqueur and comes from Milan while the other is a herbal digestif and is made in Germany. There the dissimilarities end. Both include tinctures of over forty different herbs and both taste vile beyond all belief. Imagine the fermented bile of a tubercular skunk and you are beginning to get the picture.

But go into any bar worth its salt, anywhere in the world, and there they are, lurking next to the cash register or in a corner of the top shelf, like a couple of hoods waiting to mug your hangover. Both are highly alcoholic and in moderation, quietly effective.

Chapter Eight
This Calls for a Doctor

● ● ●

So far we have heard the opinion of every know-all, smart alec and wise guy that has ever held a glass to his lips. Prehistoric peasants, syphilis-raddled monarchs, magicians, megalomaniacs, sex maniacs and dipsomaniacs, we have listened to them all. We have given them the respect they deserve and in many cases, respect they don't deserve.

But now it is time to hear from the experts, that small body of brave people whose job it is to really know what's going on in our bodies, who bring years of study and learning to the subject and who might just be telling the truth.

On the other hand they might not. Because the sad fact is that no matter how wise and good we think they are, doctors are only human. They are subject to ambition, whimsy, misplaced belief, error and downright malice, just like the rest of us.

DR LEONARD GOLDBERG'S LIBRIUM TREATMENT

Take Dr Leonard Goldberg's librium treatment as presented to the 28th International Conference on Alcohol and Alcoholism. After testing a thousand volunteers, he concluded that the tranquilliser librium cures hangovers and sobers you up twice as fast as coffee. Now that may be because coffee doesn't sober you up at all. And as any teenager who has ever raided their parents' valium bottle will tell you, tranquillizers actually enhance the effects of alcohol.

On the other hand they can help you sleep better. Sometimes for ever, as Brian Jones, Jim Morrison, Jimi Hendrix and so forth will testify - or not. On balance, it's probably best to steer clear of this one unless you are under close medical supervision.

DR MACK MITCHELL'S WORD OF ADVICE
Drink on a full stomach. This is probably the best thing you can do (besides drinking less) to reduce the severity of a hangover, says Dr Mitchell.

DR LINUS PAULING'S VITAMIN REMEDY
Nobel prize winner Dr Linus Pauling recommends massive doses of vitamin C. He is supported by Australian research which suggests that 30g of the stuff taken intravenously can sober you up within minutes, leaving you with no after-effects. Sounds good. Should work.

All I can say is that I once tried to drink 10g of dilute vitamin C, or ascorbic acid as it is more accurately known, to cure a particularly vicious hangover. It ripped into my stomach lining as if it were sulphuric acid. Within moments I was incontinent and nauseous. Hours later I had still not recovered.

DR FEELGOOD'S VITAMIN PILL CORNUCOPIA

This pillfest is closely related to Dr Pauling's remedy, but is a better-balanced cure which can be taken the night before. It should replace most of the vitamins and minerals destroyed by the booze. If nothing else your body will produce a soothing rattling noise when you walk.

Twice daily doses of vitamins A and D

Four times daily doses of vitamins B1, B6, and C

10-20mg nioxin, 250mg calcium, 250mg magnesium

DR SEYMOUTH DIAMOND'S EIGHT-STEP PROGRAMME

The last word has to go to the brilliant Dr Diamond, director of the Diamond Headache Clinic, because he tells it how it is. He brutally points out that there is no way of completely ridding yourself of a hangover. If you have poisoned your body and deprived it of sleep, it needs time to heal and you need to time to suffer.

However, there are certain things you can do to make it feel a little better:

STEP ONE

Drink fruit juice. The fructose will help you metabolise the alcohol faster.

STEP TWO

Take pain relief. A headache is one of the worst parts of a hangover.

STEP THREE

Drink water. Plenty before and after bedtime will help rehydration.

STEP FOUR

Eat amino acids to help replace the proteins destroyed by alcohol.

STEP FIVE

Drink coffee. Just two cups will reduce the swelling in your blood vessels that causes headache.

STEP SIX

Eat a good meal, but keep it light. No fats or fried foods. *Consommé* (a clear soup made from meat or chicken stock) will help replace salt and potassium.

STEP SEVEN

Take B complex vitamins. These shorten hangovers by helping your stressed body systems.

STEP EIGHT

Sleep. Go to bed early the next day. Your body can then repair itself.